I CAN READ ABOUT
PECOS BILL

Written by J.I. Anderson
Illustrated by John Killgrew

Wild Bill

Wyatt

Bat

Jesse

Billy The Kid

Kit

Many famous people
lived in the Old West.

But the most famous of all
was a rough, tough cowboy. His
name was Pecos Bill.

Pecos Bill was the smartest, the roughest,
the toughest, the most handsome, and the greatest
cowboy there ever was!

He could outride, outshoot,
and outwrangle every other cowboy
in the West.
In fact, Pecos Bill taught
the other cowboys how to ride, how
to shoot, and how to wrangle!

Bill was special. As a baby, he drank lion's
milk, and wrestled big, old grizzly bears just for fun.

Bill had to be tough. He had over a dozen brothers and sisters. He had to fight just to get enough to eat.

One day, when Bill was a baby, his father discovered that some newcomers had settled 50 miles away.

"This country's getting too crowded!" he said. So he packed up his family, and headed west towards Texas.

The wagon was very crowded.
And, wouldn't you know it . . . when the wagon
hit a bump, little Bill bounced out.
He went tumbling to the ground,
right into the dry riverbed
of the Pecos River.

The coyotes liked Bill as soon as they saw him.
They adopted him into their family. Bill learned
to be a coyote quickly.

Before long, he could outrun, outfight and outhowl
every coyote in the pack.

One day, a cowboy was riding on the prairie.
Suddenly he stopped his horse, and leaned forward in the saddle.
He couldn't believe his eyes. There was a *boy*
running with a pack of coyotes!

Bill snarled and growled at the cowboy.

"I *am* a coyote," he snapped.

"I have sharp teeth and fleas. I can run, I can fight, and I can howl."

Then he started to howl for the cowboy.

"If you're a coyote, where's your tail?" the cowboy asked.
Bill scratched his head. He didn't have a tail.
"You're a human being," the cowboy said.
Bill had to agree. So he decided
to ride with the cowboy and learn
how to be a human.

"First, you need clothes, then a horse," said the cowboy.
"No problem," answered Bill. He grabbed a bull and pulled so hard
that the bull jumped out of his skin. Bill used the skin to make
a leather suit of clothes. Then, he saw a mountain lion.
Bill grabbed the mountain lion, and talked
it into being his horse.

The cowboy took Bill to the Rusty Nail Ranch to meet
some other cowboys. But, when the cowboys saw
Bill riding a mountain lion, they turned
and ran for safety.
"Who's boss around here?"
called Bill.

A big, seven-foot-tall man stepped forward.
He was wearing three guns, and he had nine knives
hanging from his belt. But when he saw Bill, he got a bad
case of the shakes. "I-I was the boss,"
the man said, "b-but you can be the boss from now on."

Bill liked being the boss.
He had a few things he wanted to teach the
cowboys. But first he needed a *real* horse.
"I'll go out there and tame a *wild* horse,"
said Bill.

"A *wild* horse?"
The cowboys were surprised. They had never tamed
wild horses before.
"Come on, I'll show you how it's done,"
said Bill.

Bill rode out on the prairie. "There, look at that," said Bill. He pointed to a group of wild horses kicking up dust in the distance.

The lead horse was beautiful.
He looked like lightning in the sky.
He was a strong, fast stallion.
"That's the one I want," said Bill.

"Here's how to tame a wild horse," Bill cried. "First you yell '*YIPPEE,*' then you rope the horse and then you ride it." The cowboys were amazed. They had never heard of a word like *YIPPEE* and they had never heard of roping. Bill didn't have a rope, so he picked up an old rattlesnake that just happened to be curled on the ground. The rattlesnake was so shocked that its rattles fell off! Bill started swinging the snake over his head . . . round . . . and round . . . and round until the snake stretched into a long rope. Bill decided to call it a lasso.

"*Y-I-P-P-E-E*,' Bill called, as he ran after
the horse called Lightning. He tossed
the lasso around the horse's neck,
and then jumped on Lightning's back.
"*Y-I-P-P-E-E*."

Lightning didn't like having anyone on his back. He bucked and kicked as hard as he could, but Bill hung on. All day long, and all night long, Lightning bucked and kicked with all his might. But he could not throw Pecos Bill. Finally, around noon the next day, they both fell to the ground exhausted. Then they shook hands and decided to become partners.

Now that he had a horse, Bill decided to teach the cowboys a few other things. He showed them how to lasso cows. He taught them how to round up cattle. And he invented branding so the cowboys could tell which cattle belonged to them.

Pecos Bill invented the
cattle drive. That way, the
men were able to take hundreds of
cows to market at one time.

Bill had lots of bright ideas!
He invented the six-gun, the ten-gallon hat,
spurs, chaps, barbed wire, horned toads,
long-horn steers, bulldogging, bronco-busting,
and the chuck wagon.

But his best invention was the cowboy song.

Bill invented cowboy songs when he heard a group of cowboys singing songs about the sea.

"You're not sailors, you're cowboys," Bill told them. "You should be singing songs about the prairie, about cattle, and about your horses."

The cowboys became so good at roping, bulldogging, and bronco-busting that Bill had to invent the rodeo. At the rodeo, the cowboys could show off their new skills for the folks in town.

"*Y-I-P-P-E-E.*"

Bill was so busy inventing things that he hardly noticed the weather. For a long time there had been no rain in Texas. The drought had come! Things were getting so dry that the cactus drooped. The cows' tongues were hanging out. And the Rio Grande River just dried up and disappeared.

Bill had an idea. As fast as he could, Bill lassoed the water from the Gulf of Mexico to fill up the Rio Grande River. But that was not good enough. Only a big rainstorm could end the drought. Then he saw just what he needed . . . a twisting cyclone was spinning over Oklahoma.

Bill rode Lightning to Oklahoma.
He tossed up his lasso and caught the cyclone
right around its neck.

Then he climbed up on it, and rode it back to Texas.
"*Y-I-P-P-E-E*," cried Bill. The cyclone huffed
and puffed, and tried to throw Bill off.
But Bill wouldn't let go. Instead, he
started squeezing the cyclone .
He squeezed . . . and squeezed . . .
and squeezed all the rain
out of the cyclone
until it washed away
the drought.

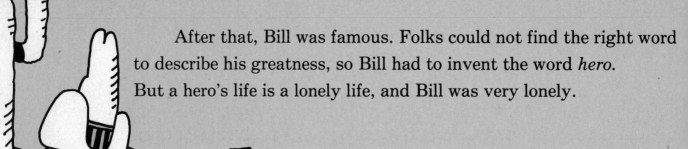

After that, Bill was famous. Folks could not find the right word
to describe his greatness, so Bill had to invent the word *hero*.
But a hero's life is a lonely life, and Bill was very lonely.

Just then, who should come riding down the Rio Grande River on
a giant catfish, but Slue-foot Sue! She was
the prettiest girl he had ever seen.
It was love at first sight, and
Bill asked her to marry him.

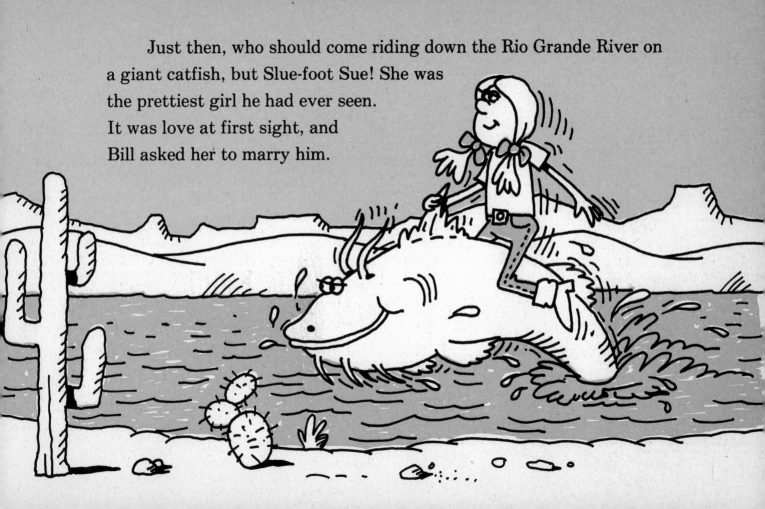

"I'll marry you, Pecos Bill," she said. "But you must promise to let me ride Lightning on our wedding night."
At first, Bill said no.

"Lightning will throw you."
But she begged and begged,

until Bill finally said yes.

On their wedding night, Sue climbed
up on Lightning's back. Lightning did not
like it one bit. He began to buck and kick . . .
harder and harder until Sue was tossed
                    up . . . up . . . up . . .
. . . all the way to the moon.

Bill got out his lasso
and tried to lasso Sue down
from the moon. But it
was no use.

"Oh, my heart is broken."
Bill cried and cried and cried.
Some folks say he cried so hard he caused
the Great Salt Lake to form in Utah.

Pecos Bill was so sad.

After that, he lost all interest in being a cowboy.

One day, he said goodbye to his men, climbed on Lightning,
    and rode off into the sunset.

The men at the Rusty Nail Ranch never saw Bill again.
But sometimes at night, they thought they saw the face of Slue-foot Sue
smiling in the moon. And sometimes, they thought they heard
the voice of Pecos Bill howling at the moon
with the coyotes.

But one thing *is* sure.
Of all the cowboys that ever lived,
Pecos Bill was the smartest,
the roughest, the toughest, and
the greatest cowboy of all.